I0797694

7

Written by Erica Fyvie
Illustrated by Scot Ritchie

Kids Can Press

To Jay, Liv and Grace, for our past, present and future — E.F.

To my grandmother Kathleen Hyslop, with memories of her one-room schoolhouse on Manitoulin Island — S.R.


## Acknowledgments

First, to my family: Loretta Fyvie, Peter Fyvie and Nicole Fyvie, and also Marzipan and Clover. To my grade school in Manhattan, P.S. 158, which was built in 1898 and served as an inspiration for Birch Elementary Public School. To my (then) Grade 6 student readers, Naio Martin and Casy Miller, for reading an early draft and giving insightful and helpful feedback. To Molly Peacock for teaching me so much about a writing life. To all of my friends for their love and support; I want to list them here, but cannot because of space. To everyone who contributed their intelligence, artistic vision, design expertise, professional support and kindness to this book. Jay, Liv and Grace Lilley, for everything, always.





Published in Canada and the U.S. by Kids Can Press Ltd.
25 Dockside Drive, Toronto, ON M5A 0B5

Kids Can Press is a Corus Entertainment Inc. company
www.kidscanpress.com

The artwork in this book was rendered in pencil, followed by line work in ink. It was then scanned into the computer and colored in Photoshop.
The text is set in Patrick Hand.

Edited by Jennifer Stokes and Kathleen Fraser
Designed by Andrew Dupuis and Marie Bartholomew

Printed and bound in Shenzhen, China, in 03/2025 by C & C Offset

CM 25 0 9 8 7 6 5 4 3 2 1

**Library and Archives Canada Cataloguing in Publication**

Title: The sustainable school : a journey through time and energy / written by Erica Fyvie; illustrated by Scot Ritchie.

Names: Fyvie, Erica, 1973– author | Ritchie, Scot, illustrator

Description: Includes bibliographical references and index.

Identifiers: Canadiana 20240521633 | ISBN 9781525306686 (hardcover)

Subjects: LCSH: Power resources — Juvenile literature. | LCSH: Renewable energy sources — Juvenile literature. | LCSH: Energy industries — Juvenile literature.

Classification: LCC TJ163.23 .F98 2025 | DDC j333.79 — dc23

Kids Can Press gratefully acknowledges that the land on which our office is located is the traditional territory of many nations, including the Mississaugas of the Credit, the Anishnabeg, the Chippewa, the Haudenosaunee and the Wendat Peoples, and is now home to many diverse First Nations, Inuit and Métis Peoples.

We thank the Government of Ontario, through Ontario Creates and the Ontario Arts Council; the Canada Council for the Arts; and the Government of Canada, for their financial support of our publishing activity.

# Contents

# Welcome to Birch Elementary

*Sustainability* means having our needs met now without compromising the ability of people in the future to meet their own needs.

Okay, let's hear from our Eco Club representatives.
Class 6

The energy audit showed that the school's furnace wastes energy by working harder when heat is lost through drafty windows.
An *energy audit* is a series of tests that analyzes a building's efficiency. It checks how well a property functions by figuring out how much energy it uses and how much energy it wastes.

The obvious solution: replace the old windows with new insulated ones to help keep heat inside in cold weather and outside in hot weather.

Nice! It's always too hot or too cold in here.

And I know you all want to hear about the new plumbing.
Water you talking about?
Ha ha!
GLASS

You know how it takes a long time for water to come out of the drinking fountain?
And how the school garden and baseball field always look kind of dead?

We're getting a rainwater collection system with a massive storage tank. It'll supply water for the school's grass, trees and other plants. That means the indoor plumbing system won't have to work as hard.

How big is "massive"?
Like, 95 000 liters or 25 000 gallons big.
The rain on the roof will be collected and sent down to the storage tank.

Except for the water needed for the green roof. We're creating a rooftop garden up there, too.
It turns out our roof is good for more than losing baseballs.

Something has got the construction workers excited.
Whoa!!

Ahem ... The green roof will have six layers.
What did they find?
*Sunshine! IT'S HAPPENING!*

1. Plants!
2. Soil or some other growing medium
3. A filter to keep plant parts from clogging the system
4. A drainage layer to prevent leaks
5. A root barrier, so roots don't poke through the top-floor ceiling
6. A waterproof membrane

Next, we'll add solar panels to help the plants grow and, eventually, to help power the school!

# Buried Treasure

How come the kids in 2000 never found it?
I've been wondering that, too.
There was a plaque marking the spot, but it's been hidden all these years. Yesterday they found the plaque near the big oak tree, and that made them dig to see what was there.

Do you want to see what's inside?
OPEN ME! OPEN ME!

Yes! Open it!
Okay, now I feel a bit shy.

We have to be careful with the contents. These are historical artifacts. They could be very fragile.
And valuable?

This appears to be a letter from the Class 6 teacher, Miss Sorman. It's dated June 1900.
Miss Sorman! Oh, she was so great.

Each spacious classroom has large windows that provide excellent ventilation and an abundance of daylight. We also have hygienic indoor plumbing facilities, with clean running water. And I am writing this letter under an electric light.

We are living in what the newspapers call a time of optimism. Our beautiful modern school reflects that sense of confidence.

In this time capsule, you will find our letters and other objects to tell you what life was like here in 1900. We have also used our school's brand-new Brownie box camera to create photographs as a visual record of our times.

What might Birch be like in the next century? Does the school look the same? Do you still use electricity for lighting? Does the plumbing still work? How do you travel to school?

We wish you a future that is peaceful, happy and full of equally interesting innovations.
Sincerely,
Miss Edna Sorman, Class 6 teacher

# The Origins of the Energy League

ELECTRICITY
PLUMBING
BUILDINGS
TRANSPORTATION

Miss Sorman asked her students to write about new and exciting developments in their daily lives. She chose four subjects: electricity, plumbing, buildings and transportation.

In a twist of magic, these are the same topics we've been covering in our energy unit because they all use or produce energy.

I like "teams"! And all the teams together can make up The Energy League!

Oh, boy.

ELECTRICITY
PLUMBING
BUILDINGS
TRANSPORTATION
But wait, there's no one interested in Team Plumbing?

Shocker!

I know, but plumbing is more than toilets. It also means watering the school grounds and baseball field. Remember? Keeping them green.

In that case, I'm Team Plumbing. Who wants in?

Riiinngg!!!

The time capsule will be here when you get back from lunch. I promise.
*I knew they'd love me!*

# School Life in 1900

**A Typical Day in the Life of Our Classroom**
by Miss Sorman's class

At the front of our school is this boot scraper. Miss Sorman says that since more and more roads are being paved, you might not recognize this. Because we walk to school mostly on dirt roads that are often muddy or worse (thank you, horses!), we must scrape our boots before walking inside.

There are 40 children in our class, and we each get our own desk and chair. Our desktops are attached to the seat of the student sitting ahead of us. We keep our books and slates inside the desk.

The woodstove keeps our class very warm in the winter. At lunchtime, we can buy a hot lunch for a penny, but most of us bring our own lunch in a metal pail. Sometimes we bring a carrot or potato to school and the midday helpers cook a stew in the school kitchen for us to share.

We have two outfits: one for school and one for worship or special occasions. Miss Sorman says that when she was a little girl, children were dressed as small adults in clothing that was starched and restrictive. She thinks we are fortunate to have more comfortable outfits.

Do you study the same subjects as we do? Miss Sorman is especially strict about penmanship. This year, we've started physiology, which is the study of the human body. Perhaps in the year 2000 you will have a cure for all diseases.

— June 1900

# Not Just a Science Fair, A Future Fair!

## Time Capsule #1: The Global Seed Vault

*Some time capsules are unplanned and accidental, like the city of Pompeii, which was trapped in time by a lava eruption in 79 CE.*

SEED BANK

**What: The Global Seed Vault**
**Where: Spitsbergen Island, Norway**
**When: 2008**
**Date discovered: TBD**

The Svalbard Global Seed Vault, located midway between the northern coast of Norway and the North Pole, is a time capsule of seeds protected by permafrost. The low temperatures and limited oxygen inside the vault help keep the seeds from aging.

The intention is to store seeds from all over the world to protect the global food supply. If there's a natural disaster or crop failure, future generations will still be able to grow crops from the 4.5 million seed samples.

Mr. Marons, what about food energy?
Like the energy food gives us, you mean?

No, the energy in food *waste*.

Yes ... Food waste can become biofuel ... hmm.
*What's biofuel?*

Uh-oh.
What?

Look. You know he's getting an idea for more work.

Listen, class. We have one final project this year: the science fair. What if we combined our work on the time capsule with that? We can stay on the same teams and explore what electricity, plumbing, buildings and transportation will look like in the future.
How?

Okay, for example, Team Electricity just asked if food waste can become fuel. Wouldn't it be great if food waste could be used to power Birch in the future?
But what can Team Transportation do?
So, it's not just a science fair — it's a future fair?
The Future Fair — yes! This time capsule has inspired us, and now we get to think about the year 2125.
Well, when you think of the future, what do you see? How are people getting around?
I don't know. Hover boards?
You're welcome.
Fantastic! Look at the science of that!

# What Is Energy?

*Kinetic energy* is the energy of motion. If we want something to move, we need to apply force to it. Applying force means we need to add work. Even moving a small ball requires the work of your hand. Now the energy in your hand has been transferred to the kinetic energy of the ball. Energy never disappears, but instead changes form.

Nice moves, Mr. M.
So that's kinetic energy!

Why can't we all just use energy-efficient things all the time? Why don't we all have solar panels?
What about the energy required to stay perfectly still? That's impressive, too!

All energy sources have some negative impacts. Even "greener" ones like solar and wind power take fuel and resources to build.

And I didn't know that electricity was powered by anything! I just saw poles and wires and thought you flipped a switch and it all just happened.

When all you do is flip a switch, it's easy to believe it just happens. We get electricity from three different sources: fossil fuels, nuclear energy and renewable energy.

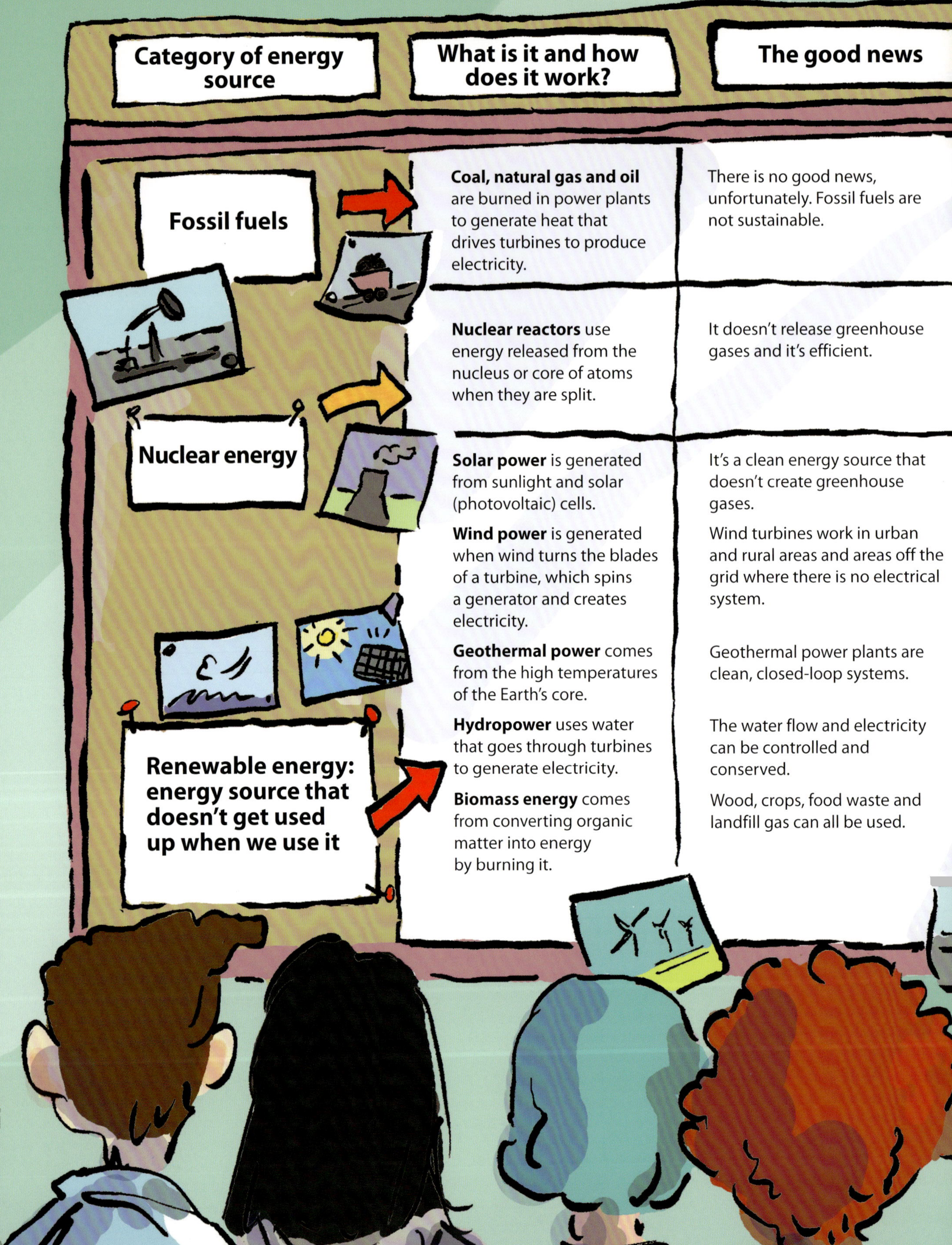

Category of energy source
What is it and how does it work?
The good news
Fossil fuels
**Coal, natural gas and oil** are burned in power plants to generate heat that drives turbines to produce electricity.
There is no good news, unfortunately. Fossil fuels are not sustainable.
Nuclear energy
**Nuclear reactors** use energy released from the nucleus or core of atoms when they are split.
It doesn't release greenhouse gases and it's efficient.
Renewable energy: energy source that doesn't get used up when we use it
**Solar power** is generated from sunlight and solar (photovoltaic) cells.
It's a clean energy source that doesn't create greenhouse gases.
**Wind power** is generated when wind turns the blades of a turbine, which spins a generator and creates electricity.
Wind turbines work in urban and rural areas and areas off the grid where there is no electrical system.
**Geothermal power** comes from the high temperatures of the Earth's core.
Geothermal power plants are clean, closed-loop systems.
**Hydropower** uses water that goes through turbines to generate electricity.
The water flow and electricity can be controlled and conserved.
**Biomass energy** comes from converting organic matter into energy by burning it.
Wood, crops, food waste and landfill gas can all be used.

The challenges
Because they're buried, we need to drill, dig, frack and deforest to get them. Then we burn them, which pollutes the air.
Nuclear reactors require uranium, which is mined and creates radioactive waste.
It's hard to count on, because fog, clouds and other weather may affect it.
The whirring blades cause noise problems for some animals and humans.
It's very expensive to install and can't be transported to another area.
Hydropower plants are expensive and destructive to plant and animal life.
Burning biomass releases greenhouse gases, and clearing land to grow crops for biofuel depletes the soil.
Okay, class. I hope you've all been *energized* by this discussion! You have everything you need to get started on your projects. Remember, I want you to share your letters from Miss Sorman's class and explain how you got your future ideas. We'll start presentations two weeks from now.
The Future Fair
Each team will research and present an idea about what kind of energy will power Birch Elementary and its students in 2125. Present your findings on a display board and include the following:
1. Project title
2. Question your group is asking about the future
3. Prediction about the answer
4. Vision for the future (how your prediction will work)
5. Some good news about your idea
6. Some challenges about your idea

# Team Electricity

I hope you have a nice life.

Sincerely,
Ethel Treadgold

P.S. There is one thing that I would like, but it's not electric. It is from my aunt's mail-order catalog: an ice cream freezer with a crank handle. It advertises the most "delicious frozen cream you have ever tasted." However, it costs $1.26.

I wonder what $1.26 equals in today's dollars?

Probably a million.

My dad is always turning off our lights. He says when we waste electricity, we burn money.

We found this story in the newspaper archive about an electrical fire in May 1900.
What happened?

A fire broke out at the Leland Blouse Department —
Blouse!

Yes, it's an old-fashioned word. Let's not interrupt.
Wait? Words go out of fashion? Do clothes?

Everyone got weirded out about electricity when a light bulb in the store window touched the clothes and started a fire.

That is scary.
But gas lanterns and wood stoves caused fires, too, right?

We tend to be more comfortable with the dangers we know. Still, it's good to question innovations.
So, tell us about your future idea and how you got it.

## *Time Capsule #2: The Terracotta Warriors*

**What: The Terracotta Warriors**
**Where: Shaanxi province, northwest China**
**When: Between 246 and 210 BCE**
**Date discovered: 1974**

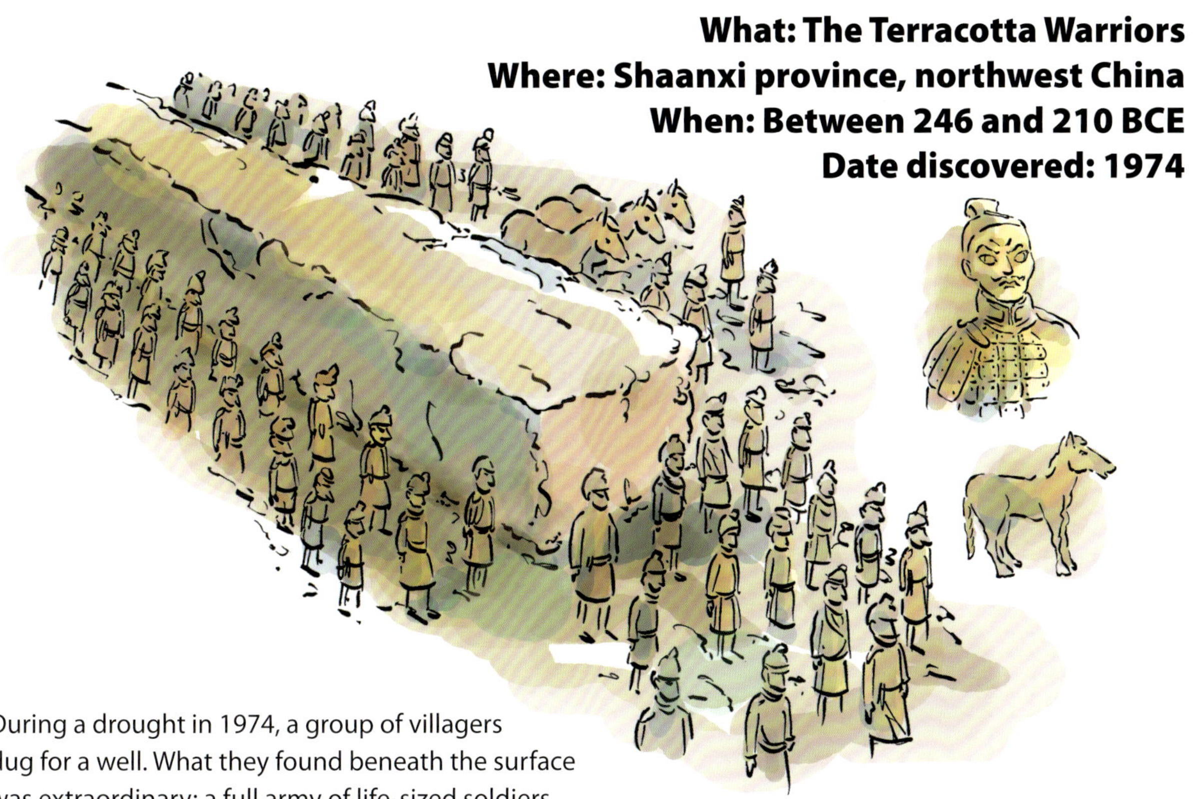

During a drought in 1974, a group of villagers dug for a well. What they found beneath the surface was extraordinary: a full army of life-sized soldiers and horses made of terracotta (fired clay) that had been buried for more than 2000 years.

It was a replica of the court of Qin Shi Huangdi, the first emperor of China. More than 8000 terracotta soldiers, 520 horses and 130 chariots have been discovered so far. No record was left of this army in any ancient scroll. However, this time capsule has provided a lot of information about military history, the ranks of warriors and even how they metal-plated swords to prevent rust.

## Question

How can we harness the energy in food waste to power our school?

## Prediction

Our school's biggest source of renewable energy in 2125 will be fuel from food waste.

### Vision for the future

1. Leftovers go into a bin.
2. The bins get trucked to a food-waste treatment station.
3. The food waste (biomass) gets mixed into a giant, goopy mess.
4. The biomass is sent to an oxygen-free digester dome.
5. Bacteria breaks down the food waste.
6. The biofuel created from this process is methane, which is injected into the pipeline to power electricity.
7. Food waste now = resource later.

*This is incredible! It's as if I've landed in my own Land of Oz.*

# Leftovers for Fuel

## The good news

- The food-waste treatment station can create one megawatt of electricity per hour, enough to power the school, its buses and the trucks that transport the food waste.
- If we treat food waste as a resource, it stays out of landfills. In landfills, food waste still creates methane, but it just releases into the atmosphere.
- Since everyone eats, we hope that all schools can use this technology for electricity.

## The challenges

- It requires a lot of energy to power food-waste treatment stations. We hope that in the future they will run on solar power or some other alternative energy.
- We hope this won't make kids think that food waste is no big deal. Even if we use it as fuel, it's not good to waste food, because a lot of resources already go into making and transporting it.
- Composting food waste is valuable for the soil, so we want to continue composting.

## Conclusion

Because all sources of energy have an impact on the environment, we think the future will be about using the least harmful ones.

# Team Plumbing

Birch Elementary has an indoor bathroom on each floor.

At home we use a privy out back. For baths, we pump water from the well, heat it in the kettle and add it to the washtub. I'm the youngest of four children in my house, which means my bath happens after everyone else's in the same water. That's as much fun as it sounds.

Miss Sorman is very enthusiastic about sanitation and hygiene. She thinks indoor plumbing is essential for keeping us alive. (I wouldn't go that far.) We have lessons in properly blowing our nose and washing our hands.

The Health Board sends schools a list of all houses where there is contagious disease. Mr. Webster, our principal, looks at his register, and anyone from a contagious house has to be excluded from school. Miss Sorman thinks that if everyone had indoor plumbing, fewer students would miss school because of illness.
HEALTH BOARD

My parents think indoor plumbing is dangerous and sewer gases can come up through the toilets and sinks. My mother told me not to go to the bathroom at school. I promised, but crossed my fingers behind my back. So far, no one in my class has perished due to sewer vapors.

I hope you do not have to write about indoor plumbing in the year 2000, and that our school has a really good baseball team by then.
Yours truly,
John Massey
BIRCH
ELEMENTARY

## Clean water in, wastewater out

Miss Sorman was right! Indoor plumbing is directly connected to preventing disease. Before water pipes made indoor plumbing possible, people collected fresh water and dumped bathroom waste at the same place. By 1900, new water and sewer networks were carrying clean water in and wastewater out. These sanitation measures helped to keep people healthy.

Then we got an idea. Ms. Rabia was outside with the kindergarteners. When we told her what we were working on, she looked at her students running around and said, "Too bad you can't bottle up their energy!"

## *Time Capsule #3: The Wreck of the* Titanic

**What: The Wreck of the *Titanic***

**Where: At the bottom of the Atlantic Ocean**

**When: April 14, 1912**

**Date discovered: September 1, 1985**

The wreck of the *Titanic* is an unplanned time capsule. The ship sank on April 14, 1912, and the wreck wasn't discovered for 73 years. More than 5500 artifacts were recovered. One item was a pocket watch, frozen in time at 2:16. This helped determine exactly when the ship plunged into the water.

A piece of the steel hull of the ship was recovered in 1998. Scientists realized that the steel used in the *Titanic* was much more brittle than the steel used in modern ships. This helps plan for safer engineering techniques today.

## Question

Can the kinetic energy of students pump water for the school?

## Prediction

Birch's future playground will capture and store its students' kinetic energy. That energy will be used to pump water into the school. No water will be wasted, and kids will be more active. And there will still be room to play baseball!

### Vision for the future

Underneath the paved and grassy areas of the Birch playground, there will be motion-activated pads. When the students go out for recess and run around, the weight of their footsteps will react with the pads. The pads will read and store the kinetic energy of all the kids every day. Once the energy hits a certain level, it will be enough to pump water into the pipes that go into the school.

When the students get thirsty after all that running around, it'll be their energy that activates the water to flow out of the water fountains inside. A perfect system!

## Move It … to Drink It!

### The good news

- During winter break and summer vacation, there won't be kids playing and activating the pads. That's okay, because there will only be a small number of people at the school and enough kinetic energy stored to give them the water they need. This will cut down on energy waste for when Birch is mostly empty.
- It will save water *and* conquer laziness!

### The challenges

None! Maybe getting the system up and running will be expensive, but it will save the school a fortune over time.

## Conclusion

Working for our water will be the way of the future and we'll feel better for it!

# Team Buildings

Hello!

My assignment is to express how fine our new school building is.

I think it looks dignified and refined, very proper and clean. Miss Sorman said it was built in a beaux arts style and is intended to suggest the kind of learning we will do inside.

There are large windows in all the classrooms, and our desks all face the same way to allow the most sunlight to fall over our left shoulders. This is because we are all expected to write with our right hand.

My very best friend, Ethel, has already written about electricity. We use the electric lights only when it is dark outside.

This is not just an exciting time for our school, but also for our hometown. My father works downtown in a building that has an actual passenger elevator! It's the Lilley & Ellis Insurance building. He still takes the stairs every day, but promises that one day he will try the elevator lift. Once he deems it safe, I will be able to try it, too. I already know how it will feel — like floating.
LILLEY + ELLIS INSURANCE

He said that the new buildings going up downtown are called "skyscrapers" because it looks as if they scrape the sky. Some are ten stories high! Isn't that marvelous?

The building where my father works is partly made of steel, which is expensive, but lasts forever. That means it will still be downtown when you read this!

I turn 12 on June 14, so I look forward to meeting you when I am 112!
Sincerely,
Gwen Lilley

A *retrofit* adds something that adapts or improves. For Birch, that means upgrading to increase the building's energy efficiency.

## *Time Capsule #4: Voyager Golden Records*

**What: Voyager Golden Records**

**Where: On *Voyager 1* and *Voyager 2*, twin spacecraft currently somewhere in interstellar space**

**When: Launched in 1977**

**Date discovered: TBD**

The Golden Records are phonograph records that contain sounds and images of life on Earth. They are intended to teach any extraterrestrial life forms that may find them about the diversity of our life and culture.

The records contain greetings in 55 languages, 90 minutes of music and 12 minutes of specific Earth sounds, including a whale song, a kiss and brain waves. Images include photographs of huts, houses and cityscapes, and an illustration of humans' DNA structure. Scientists expect the records to be discovered in 40 000 years, but it's hard to guarantee interstellar space travel arrival times!

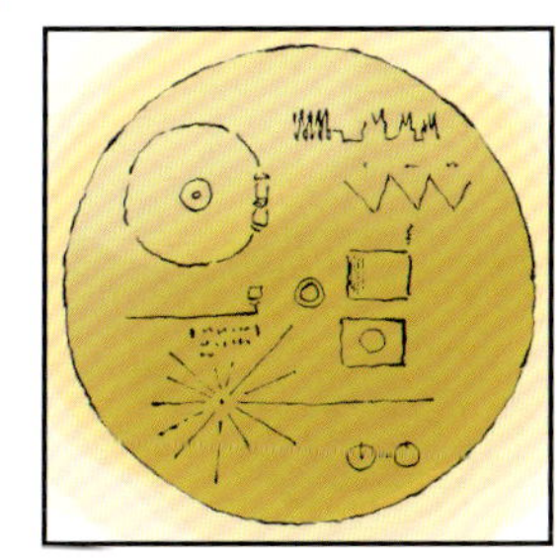

## Question

Can we build a new building with only recycled materials?

## Prediction

By the year 2125, any new construction at Birch will be built with plastic bricks made from recycled materials.

### Vision for the future

1. Plastic will be collected and sent to our school's sorting station.
2. The station will be made of plastic bricks, powered by food-waste fuel (biofuel) and run by robots!
3. The containers will be shredded and pressed into a brick-shaped mold.
4. The plastic bricks will be like toy building blocks, with grooves that click into place to hold them together.
5. Birch will use them for new construction on the school property.
6. The school will also sell the recycled plastic bricks as a moneymaker!

# Building by Plastic?!

## The good news

- Plastic is a waterproof material and easy to mold. It's perfect for shaping into bricks.
- Each brick will require 1.58 kg (3½ lbs.) of plastic.
- Scientists already working on developing plastic bricks have discovered that they can make them in almost any color. Maybe we could make any new additions to Birch green!

## The challenges

- If we create a good use for plastic (like building materials), it's possible no one will think it's a bad idea to use so much of it.
- We still produce way more plastic than we could ever use up, and the extras fill up our oceans and landfills.

## Conclusion

We couldn't believe how much plastic we use every day: toothbrushes, running shoes, lunch bags, binders, laptops, water bottles, gum wrappers … almost everything. Picturing a future without plastic is almost impossible. Our team thinks that's the reason why it's so important to find ways to reuse it.

# Team Transportation

I have never been in one of the new "automobiles," or horseless carriages, but I saw one once. They are rare in our city, but the newspapers are certainly excited about them. Even though only rich people can afford them, I predict that someday automobiles will be very popular. Your streets must be so clean without horse manure!

Sincerely,
Douglas Fraser

In 1900, most people traveled by walking or by horse and buggy. Vehicles were so slow that you could walk across the street wherever you wanted.

Bicycles and horse-and-buggy delivery carts, like Mr. Whalen's, delivered coal, ice, milk, bread and other groceries.

Douglas mentioned electric streetcars. People used them to get to work, shop and socialize. That contributed to the growth of cities. In the 1910s, some cities got buses. After that, *all* cities got cars.

And now, most of us get driven to school instead of walking.

## Time Capsule #5: Scott's Hut

**What: Scott's Hut**

**Where: Cape Evans, Ross Island, Antarctica**

**When: Built in 1911**

**Date discovered: 1956**

In 1910, Captain Robert Falcon Scott left London with a team of explorers to return to Antarctica. He had been there in 1902 and had come close to discovering the South Pole, but had to turn back.

He planned this next trip for success. In addition to tons of food, scientific equipment and fuel — plus 33 Siberian dogs — the ship carried prefabricated huts, which the explorers put together as one large hut once they arrived in Antarctica in 1911.

After much preparation, the explorers left for an expedition to the South Pole in 1912. They finally made it, only to find that another crew had discovered it first. Dejected, Scott's crew began the trip back to their hut. They never returned. The explorers faced blizzards, whiteout conditions and starvation, and died on the trip back.

In 1956, adventurers discovered Scott's hut covered in snow and ice. When they finished digging it out, they found a well-preserved time capsule. It looked as if the 1911 explorers had left just moments before. Tins of food, flipped-open magazines, clothing, bunk beds, worn boots and scientific test tubes were left frozen in time.

## Question

Is zero-fuel transportation possible?

## Prediction

In 2125, we will be living in the Age of Magnetism.

### Vision for the future

A *magnet* is a rock or a piece of metal that can pull certain types of metal toward it. *Magnetism*, or the force of magnets, works over a distance. This means that a magnet does not have to be touching an object to pull it.

### What's a *superconductor*?

A *conductor* is a material (for example, copper, silver or gold) that can transport electricity. Sometimes when an electrical device has been running for a while, the cord gets hot — the wires can't resist the flow of electricity forever, the same way we can only hold something heavy for so long. However, a *superconductor* (such as aluminum) can conduct electricity without losing energy. A superconductor works a bit like sliding something across a sheet of ice: there's no friction or resistance.

## Gliding Into the Future

### How it will work
### (We worked hard to figure this out!)

- Our hover skateboard will have a magnet at the bottom.
- Roads will have a superconductor track.
- The skateboard magnet will activate a current in the superconductor track that will allow it to hover.
- It could also allow for two tracks: some vehicles on the road and some hovering above!

### The challenge

- Superconductors work only at a very low temperature. Those underground wires will have to be very cold for the skateboard to hover. How cold? Try -178°C (-288°F). *Brrr!* Researchers wonder if liquid hydrogen can do it.

## Conclusion

There's good news: Maglev (magnetic levitation) trains already exist! Just as Douglas was excited about automobiles, we are excited about this science. We think zero-fuel travel will be possible.

# What Is Our Legacy?

Future garbologists will study our landfills and learn all about us. The layers that pile up over the years show what a community values and what it consumes. And think about all the energy it took to make those things, just for them to be thrown away.

So a landfill is like a time capsule?

Yes! It's our past and our present, too, because we make so much waste.

What about the future?

Because they take so long to decompose, landfills will outlive us. Nature figured out how to use everything and not create extra, but humans have not.

That's a pretty disappointing time capsule. What can we leave for the future besides garbage?

I'd leave my gold medal from track and field day.

I'd leave my report card.
Why would future generations want your report card?
Because I'm going to be super famous and it'll be worth something.

Can we make our own time capsule like Miss Sorman's class did?
That's a brilliant idea!

*Welcome to the Museum of ME!*
TIME CAPSULE

Dear future Class 6,
When you read this, we will be more than 90 years old. That's hard to imagine! We put our full names here, so you can find us in the future. We hope to visit in person via magnetized travel to tell you about our lives so long ago.
We found a time capsule from 1900 by chance and want to make sure that you definitely open ours.
We think that understanding the energy needs of our school today can help your school tomorrow. What awaits you (and us) in the future? Maybe there will be underwater schools you get to via submarine? Maybe teachers will be holograms! Whatever happens, if you're reading this, you're alive in a time that will surely be filled with wonder.
Our school's gardener told us that birch trees can live for hundreds of years under good conditions. If they don't get the right water or sun, they have a short life. We hope our Birch Elementary has the optimal conditions for survival.
We are looking forward to meeting you in the future!
Mr. Maron's Class 6, 2025
Report Card
BIRCH ELEMENTARY
GOLD
BIRCH ELEMENTARY LUNCH MENU
CHICKEN TANDOORI
VEGGIE PIZZA
BIRCH STEW
TRIPLE SANDWICH
I'm going underground, people! Mark my place well. Here's hoping everyone doesn't live on Mars in 2125, because then I'll really be waiting ...
2025

Birch Elementary Public School, 2125
Playground:
Kids playing baseball are generating more kinetic energy than the kids sitting underneath the tree.
Vehicle storage:
Hover boards levitate against the front wall of the school.
Greenhouse:
The plastic brick greenhouse next to the sorting station grows plants used for school lunches all year round.
HOVER
Time capsule:
The 2025 time capsule is buried here, to be opened the last week of school in 2125!
Electricity:
A truck run by food waste leaves the property to go to the food-waste treatment station.
GREENHOUSE
SORTING
RUNS ON FOOD WASTE

# BIRCH ELEMENTARY CLASS 6, 2025

DAWN

AUGUST

HORACE

OMAR

SUMMER

IDAN

NEEMA

DELANO

ELAM

CHEN

MIRAI

VERNA

# CREATE YOUR OWN TIME CAPSULE

**Here are some ideas on what to write about and to include in your time capsule.**

**Personal Time Capsule**

- My best friend
- My favorite snack
- My favorite team(s)
- My favorite thing to read
- What I like to eat for breakfast/lunch/dinner
- Best movie I've seen
- Clothes I like to wear

**Include:**

- A birthday card or letter from someone I love
- A (clean and empty!) wrapper of my favorite snack(s)
- A photo of my bedroom and photos of my neighborhood

**Family Time Capsule**

- How we celebrate birthdays and holidays
- A list of chores/responsibilities we share at home
- Predict what the future holds for everyone in the family

**Include:**

- An image of our family tree
- Take-out menus for places we like to eat together
- Photos and details about family pets

**Class Time Capsule**

- What we do on the first and last day of school
- The best field trip this year
- What we do for class parties
- The subjects we studied

**Include:**

- A note from the principal or head of school
- Images of artwork from the school year
- A class photo
- Photos of our classroom, school library, grounds, lunchroom
- If the school has a lunch program, include a menu

Decide as a class where you should put it and how you should mark it so it can be found in the future.

Maybe your time capsule will have a theme, too — about energy or something else. Maybe not. Either way, just imagine future students discovering what life was like in the "old days"!

# GLOSSARY

**artifacts:** objects made by humans, such as tools, clothing and art, or the remains of those objects

**biofuel:** fuel made from biomass, usually liquid or gas

**biomass:** renewable organic matter from plants and animals, usually solid

**decompose:** to separate or break apart

**DNA:** a complex material in the cells of every living thing that contains all the information about how it will look and function

**electricity:** the flow of electrical power or charge

**energy:** the capacity for doing work

**energy audit:** a series of tests performed to understand the energy efficiency of a building

**fossil fuels:** coal, natural gas and oil

**garbologist:** a scientist who studies human society by analyzing its waste

**geothermal energy:** geo (earth) + thermal (heat) is energy extracted from the Earth's core

**greenhouse gases:** gases, such as carbon dioxide and methane, that trap heat in the atmosphere and contribute to global warming

**hologram:** a three-dimensional image generated by light beams

**hover board:** a board for personal transportation. It's like a skateboard, but it glides above the ground instead of using wheels.

**hygiene:** the practice of keeping yourself and your environment clean to maintain health

**incandescent:** white or glowing with tremendous heat

**interstellar space:** the space in a galaxy that doesn't have stars or planetary systems

**kinetic energy:** the energy of motion

**landfill:** a system for garbage disposal in which waste materials are buried or built up in layers and sometimes covered with soil

**legacy:** what one person or generation leaves behind for the next generation

**microchip:** tiny computer chip containing electrical circuits that store information

**nuclear energy:** energy released from the core (nucleus) of an atom

**penmanship:** the quality and style of handwriting

**permafrost:** ground that stays frozen at 0°C (32°F) for at least two years

**privy:** outdoor toilet

**renewable energy:** energy that doesn't deplete when we use it

**sanitation:** public health measures to provide clean drinking water and to safely deal with human waste

**sewer:** underground pipes that take away human waste and dirty water to a treatment plant

**slate:** a thin, flat piece of stone, usually in a wooden frame, that can be written on with chalk or shale pencils

**solar panel:** device used to convert the energy of the sun into electricity

**sustainability:** meeting our needs in a lasting, responsible way that does not harm the ability of people in the future to meet their own needs

**time capsule:** a planned collection of items hidden away for future discovery, or an unplanned or accidental collection of objects that tell us something important about history

**turbine:** an engine that turns movement into energy

**waste:** anything we throw away or get rid of

**work:** the amount of energy it takes to move something

# RESOURCES

**READ!**

***Past***

Editors of Time-Life Books. *This Fabulous Century 1870–1970.* Time-Life Books, 1970.

***Present***

"A Young Person's Guide to Sustainable Energy." United Nations Children's Fund (UNICEF). www.unicef.org/lac/media/40516/file/A-young-persons-guide-to-sustainable-energy.pdf.

***Future***

Kaku, Michio. *Physics of the Future: How Science Will Shape Human Destiny and Our Daily Lives by the Year 2100.* Anchor Books, 2012.

**WATCH!**

***Past***

"Back in Time for Dinner." CBC Canada video series, 2018: www.cbc.ca/life/backintimefordinner.

***Present***

NASA Climate Kids: www.climatekids.nasa.gov/menu/watch/.

***Future***

"Garbology and Our Future – Anita Zavodska." TEDx BarryU Talk, March 2020: youtu.be/m9qR2_67xaQ.

**EXPLORE!**

***Past***

Smithsonian Education Time Capsule Collection, National Postal Museum, Smithsonian Learning Lab: www.learninglab.si.edu/collections/time-capsules/xRes2nXErGagufvW.

***Present***

Our World in Data, Global Change Data Lab: www.ourworldindata.org.

***Future***

BBC Future: www.bbc.com/future/article/20151016-welcome-to-a-home-for-the-insatiably-curious/w.

# INDEX